New Persp

Arranged by Michael Kocour

This collection contains some of my favorite standards that have influenced my playing over the years. "Body and Soul" and "Stardust" were among the first jazz ballads I ever heard. While so many great artists have recorded these tunes, it is Art Tatum's virtuosic renditions on *Solo Masterpieces* that have probably influenced me the most. "Sweet Lorraine" was another of Tatum's favorites. I started playing that tune in $\frac{5}{4}$ just to change things up a bit, and I share that interpretation with you in this collection. The Riverside recordings of Bill Evans are where I discovered Cole Porter's "Ev'rything I Love." I find it hard to escape Evans's brilliant influence whenever I play this tune. Hank Jones's fantastic solo recording of "Have You Met Miss Jones?" is one of my favorite recordings by one of my all-time favorite pianists. I was also inspired by Jones's beautiful trio arrangement of "Love Walked In." Although I never found a recording of Jones playing "Poor Butterfly," I always thought that tune fit his style, and I believe my arrangement reflects that. I have many fond memories of playing Jule Styne's "Just In Time" with saxophonist Eric Schneider in Chicago. My arrangement puts the focus on the left hand, which I find to be a refreshing change of pace from time to time. I hope you enjoy exploring these arrangements, and that they in turn influence your own playing style.

—Michael Kocour

Body and Soul 2

Ev'rything I Love 8

Have You Met Miss Jones? 14

Just In Time 19

Love Walked In 26

Poor Butterfly 32

Stardust 38

Sweet Lorraine 45

GERSHWIN®, GEORGE GERSHWIN® and IRA GERSHWIN™
Are Registered Trademarks of Gershwin Enterprises

Produced by
Alfred Music Publishing Co., Inc.
P.O. Box 10003
Van Nuys, CA 91410-0003
alfred.com

Printed in USA.

ISBN-10: 0-7390-7670-1
ISBN-13: 978-0-7390-7670-5

BODY AND SOUL

Words by Edward Heyman, Robert Sour and Frank Eyton
Music by John Green
Arr. Michael Kocour

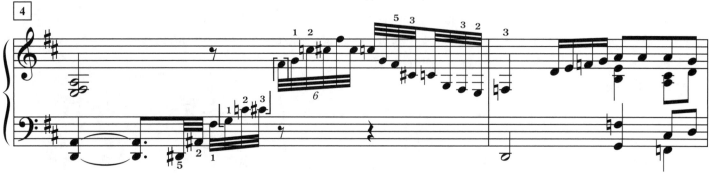

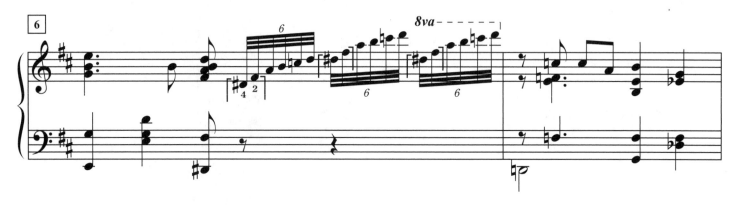

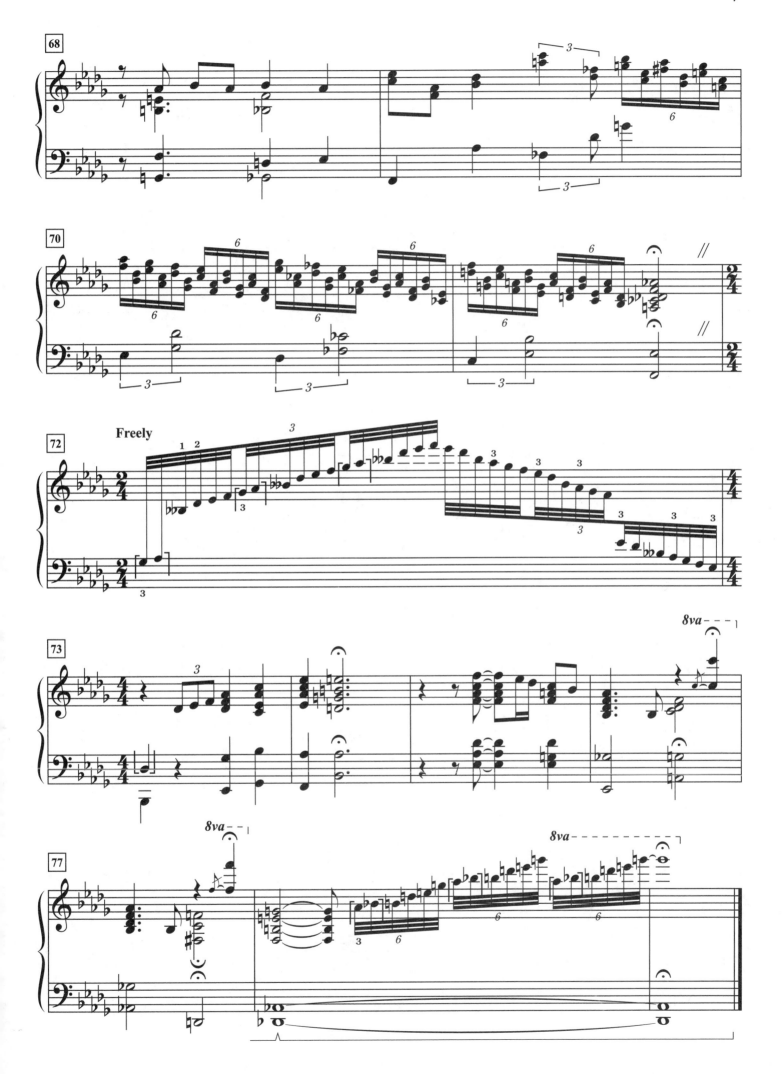

Ev'rything I Love

Words and Music by Cole Porter
Arr. Michael Kocour

HAVE YOU MET MISS JONES?

Words by Lorenz Hart
Music by Richard Rodgers
Arr. Michael Kocour

Just In Time

Lyrics by Betty Comden and Adolph Green
Music by Jule Styne
Arr. Michael Kocour

20

(roll when necessary)

Love Walked In

Music and Lyrics by George Gershwin and Ira Gershwin
Arr. Michael Kocour

Poor Butterfly

Words by John L. Golden
Music by Raymond Hubbell
Arr. Michael Kocour

STARDUST

Music by Hoagy Carmichael
Words by Mitchell Parish
Arr. Michael Kocour

Sweet Lorraine

Music by Cliff Burwell
Words by Mitchell Parish
Arr. Michael Kocour

50